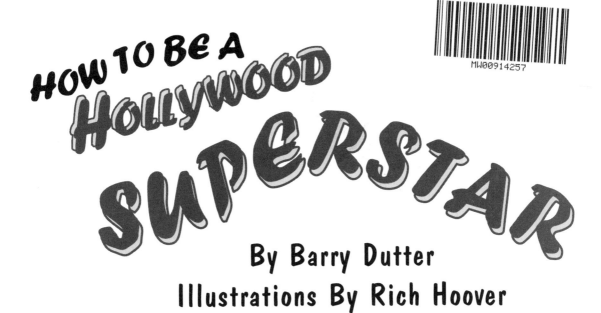

HOW TO BE A Hollywood SUPERSTAR

By Barry Dutter
Illustrations By Rich Hoover

GPG

GENERAL PUBLISHING GROUP

Los Angeles

PUBLISHER: W. QUAY HAYS
MANAGING EDITOR: COLBY ALLERTON
PRODUCTION DIRECTOR: NADEEN TORIO
PROJECTS MANAGER: TRUDIHOPE SCHLOMOWITZ
COLOR & PRE-PRESS DIRECTOR: BILL CASTILLO
PRODUCTION ASSISTANT: TOM ARCHIBEQUE
ILLUSTRATIONS: RICH HOOVER

FOR INFORMATION:
GENERAL PUBLISHING GROUP
2701 OCEAN PARK BOULEVARD, SUITE 140
SANTA MONICA, CA 90405

PRINTED IN THE USA
10 9 8 7 6 5 4 3 2 1

GENERAL PUBLISHING GROUP
LOS ANGELES

DEDICATION & ACKNOWLEDGMENTS

I'd like to dedicate this book to all the people who didn't make it into my first book: to my best friend Charlie...to my sister Valerie and her husband Richard...to my nieces and nephews, Ryan, AJ, Ashley, and Kevin...

...and I'd like to re-dedicate it to everyone I did include last time: to Tom Diaz (Go Splooge!)...to Rick Parker, who brilliantly illustrated my first book (Everything I Really Need To Know I Learned From Television—Applause Books, $7.95)...to my cousins, Nancy the poolshark, Anna & John, my aunt Mary and Uncle Jimmy, Maria & Carl, Vinnie & Molly, Donnie & Elaine, Darlene & Roy, and the entire Emiliani Family...to my pals Warren Mateychak, John Salerno & Janet Stadelmeier, Dave, Alysa, & Cullen McCormick, Ray Padolla, Bill & Mary Baker, and David Polito (who I stole a joke or two from)...to my family: Brian, Shannon, Susan, Michelle, Allison, and yes, once again, to my parents, Ray and RoseMarie—because you just can't dedicate enough books to your parents!

—Barry Dutter

I'd like to dedicate this book to my cat, Newton.　　　　—Rich Hoover

We'd also like to acknowledge the following people who helped in the production of this book: Joe Ajlouney, Dan Carr, Glenn Greenberg, Scott Lobdell, Jim Salicrup, Ian Jeffrey, Mark Jeffrey, Steve Zeber.

Whine about how nobody
understands you, and how everybody
has the completely wrong image
about you. Say things like,
"The public confuses me with
the characters I play."

If you are a grunge rocker, complain about how you hate getting all that attention. This will get you even more attention! (It works for Pearl Jam!)

If there is a war going on, make a big deal about going over to the war zone. Once you get there, make a statement about how war is a bad thing.

GET A REALLY BAD HAIRCUT.

SOME SATISFIED CUSTOMERS...

Hire a shady manager to lose or steal all your money. Make sure you follow his advice for investing in bad stocks. Then complain that you were ripped off.

15

If you're ever accused of a crime, write a book about it, and hold a bidding war for the movie rights!

DO COMMERCIALS FOR AS MANY PRODUCTS AS IS HUMANLY POSSIBLE. REMEMBER, THERE'S NO SUCH THING AS "SELLING OUT" IF YOU HAVE NO INTEGRITY TO BEGIN WITH!

If you are a former child star, make sure you go crazy or have some weird problems. (We personally recommend holding up a video store and then coming back for your sunglasses!)

Marry into a presidential family. That's always a good way to gain some respectability!

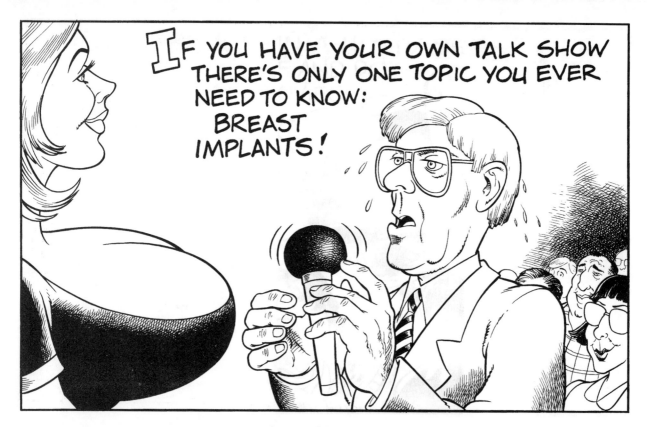

IF YOU HAVE YOUR OWN TALK SHOW THERE'S ONLY ONE TOPIC YOU EVER NEED TO KNOW: BREAST IMPLANTS!

Lend your name to a
restaurant chain that you actually
have nothing to do with!

If you are ready to get married,
just remember three little words:
pre-nuptial, pre-nuptial,
pre-nuptial!

If you are a former Charlie's Angel, do at least one TV movie where you are beaten, battered, or otherwise abused.

Do one flop TV series after another. Try and rack up the record for most failed shows!

How to be a successful female talk-show host: sympathize with your guests and cry a lot! How to be a successful male talk-show host: wear a dress every once in a while!

Sleep in an oxygen tank!

If you have a fatal disease,
tell everyone that there is nothing
wrong with you. Keep insisting that
you're fine, even up until your death.

Start a rumor that you died.
Then go on a TV talk show and
prove that you're still alive.

Become a hermit. Stay at home for months at a time. Don't go out, and don't talk to anyone. This will add to your aura of mystery.

If you want to break up with your girlfriend, do it by fax or Fed-Ex—never in person! That's the way the really hip people do it these days!

At least one drunk driving incident
is essential to being a real
Hollywood superstar.

If you're not famous, have sex with somebody who is famous. This, in turn, will make you famous, and you can spend the rest of your life talking about it.

CRUISE THE SUNSET STRIP AND PICK UP A HOOKER! MAKE SURE THE COPS CATCH YOU AND YOU WILL BECOME AN OVERNIGHT SENSATION!

If there are rumors about your being gay, marry one of the hottest young starlets in Hollywood and start cranking out lots of babies!

Start off doing porno movies at age fifteen. Then make the switch to real acting, and whine about your image of being a sex star.

Sue one of the tabloids for writing a juicy story about you—or at least threaten to.

61

If you're dating someone who is not in show business, dump them for someone who is—preferably the co-star of your latest movie. For maximum publicity, dump your spouse who you've been married to for twenty or thirty years for some hot young starlet or belly dancer.

THE MINUTE YOU HIT THE BIG-TIME, TRADE YOUR OLD WIFE IN FOR A NEW MODEL!

Pose for the covers on a bunch of romance novels. Then write a romance novel of your own—even if you can't speak English! People will buy it just for the cover!

If you are rich, and don't know what to buy your wife, a Golden Globe Award makes a lovely gift.

REMEMBER, THERE'S NO SUCH THING AS BAD PUBLICITY! NO MATTER WHAT YOU DO, THE AMERICAN PUBLIC WILL FORGIVE YOU!

Build a petting zoo on your property, and stock it with all kinds of exotic animals, especially llamas.

If you want to make the cover
of *People* magazine, you might want
to consider some sort of eating
disorder, like anorexia or bulimia.

Always flee a crime scene in a white Ford Bronco. Make sure you drive real slowly, so the TV cameras can follow your every move!

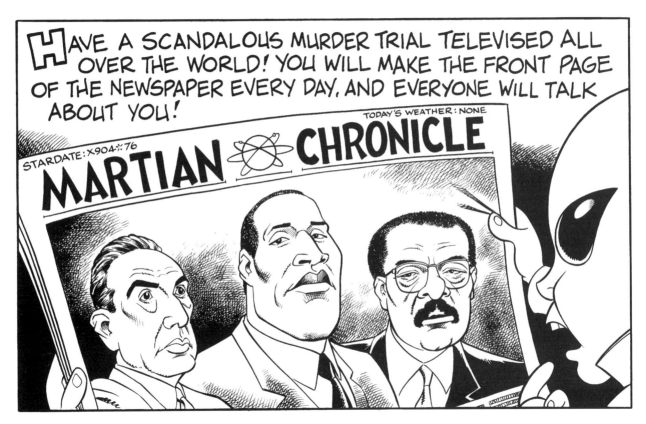

Make a sexy home video with some underage girls; try to get the video on "Hard Copy."

GO TO AN X-RATED THEATRE BY YOURSELF AND "ENJOY THE MOVIE". MAKE SURE SOME UNDER-COVER COPS ARE WATCHING YOU!

POSE NUDE FOR "PLAYBOY." THEN PUT ON A LOT OF WEIGHT AND MARRY AN AGING TEXAS BILLIONAIRE. YOUR ADDED POUNDS WILL SURELY CRUSH HIM TO DEATH IN NO TIME, THUS ENSURING YOUR FINANCIAL FUTURE!

If you are a member of the British royal family, frolic topless with someone you are not married to, and make sure the pictures get published in the tabloids.

IF YOU ARE ABOUT TO BE FIRED FROM A JOB, MAKE A BIG ANNOUNCEMENT ABOUT HOW YOU HAVE "QUIT" THE JOB.

If you really want some attention, go on TV dressed up like Catwoman. If the Catwoman thing doesn't work, develop a fatal attraction to one of your co-stars, and send voodoo dolls to his work.

If you are unpopular, try to pick
a very public fight with someone
who is more popular than you are.
In this way, you will boost
your own popularity.

If you are already famous, go to college and claim that you want to be treated "just like all the other students."

If you star on a critically-acclaimed, highly-rated TV show, quit that show and go off to do your own crappy series instead!

IF YOU HAVE EVER STARRED ON A POPULAR TV SERIES, WRITE A BOOK IN WHICH YOU DISH DIRT ON YOUR CO-STARS. THEN YOUR CO-STARS CAN ALL WRITE BOOKS ABOUT YOU.

If you are a child actress, let your showbiz mom control every facet of your career. Make a public announcement about your virginity.

REMEMBER TO ALWAYS DO SOMETHING SHOCKING WHEREVER YOU GO. THAT'S THE KEY TO STAYING FAMOUS-- IT'S ALL ABOUT SHOCKING PEOPLE.

If you are a model, complain that your job is really boring, and that it doesn't take any intelligence.

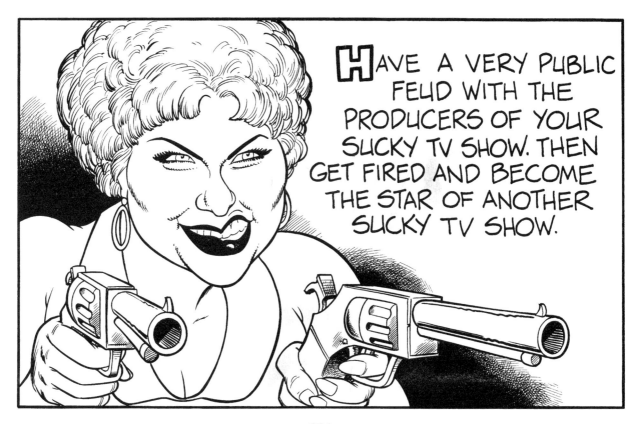

IF YOU'RE A SOAP OPERA STAR, GET NOMINATED FOR THE DAYTIME EMMY AWARDS FOURTEEN TIMES, AND LOSE EVERY TIME! THIS WILL CREATE AN INCREDIBLE AMOUNT OF SYMPATHY FOR YOU AND YOU WILL BECOME THE MOST POPULAR DAYTIME TV STAR EVER!

You have to have at least one illegitimate child. All the really big superstars do.

If you see a town you like,
buy it! If a town isn't enough for
you, buy a whole island!

Make sure you have lots of
helicopters and news photographers
at your wedding reception.

If you are a rapper, make up a phony past about yourself being raised on the streets, hanging out with gangs, etc. This will make you seem tougher, and legitimize you within the rap community!

IF YOU'RE A STAR IN A HIT TV SERIES, QUIT THE SHOW AND GO OFF AND DO SOME REALLY SUCKY MOVIES.

Want to make some big bucks? Hook up with some senile old lady who used to be a big Broadway star. Marry her, get her to re-write her will, then wait for her to kick the bucket! You may have to wait a few years, but the pay-off will be worth it!

Tape record some raunchy phone conversations, then start up your own phone-sex line.

Want to make some headlines?
Lead the cops on a high-speed car
chase through three states.
Do some time in jail, and then
make a big stink about how they
won't let you out!

Announce you are going to marry one of Hollywood's hottest actresses. Then cancel the wedding and take up with a topless dancer instead.

Make a real steamy movie that gets an NC-17 rating. Then cut it or re-shoot it so it gets an "R." This is a great attention-getter.